MEN ON A MISSION

Name	
Address	
Phone	**Email**
	www.highquest.info

HIGHQUEST - His Nature

V 5

ACKNOWLEDGEMENTS

HIGHQUEST DESIGN TEAM: Ron Bennett, Larry Glabe, Chuck Strittmatter, Bob Walz

www.HighQuest.info

HIGHQUEST : HIS NATURE

The Quest

A "quest" could be defined as a "journey with adventure". Following Christ is the ultimate quest; it is more than just a trip. In a trip, like a vacation, we leave from point A, travel to point B, and return back to point A. Along the way, we take pictures, buy souvenirs, and share experiences. A trip creates memories but not changed lives.

A quest involves leaving point A and heading to point B without making plans to return. A quest results in life change. We never recover from a quest.

Following Christ is a journey that involves both leaving what is behind and pressing on to what is ahead.

> *Can Real Men Walk With a Real God in a Real World?*

Our journey of faith in Christ does more than make memories; it involves adventure. It is a journey with drama. There is nothing boring about following Christ in His kingdom. Adventure, drama, beauty, excitement, and hardship are part of the high quest of following Christ for a lifetime. You are invited to take your next step in this exciting journey.

"In light of all this, here's what I want you to do. .. I want you to get out there and walk—better yet, run!—on the road God called you to travel. I don't want any of you sitting around on your hands. I don't want anyone strolling off, down some path that goes nowhere. And mark that you do this with humility and discipline—not in fits and starts, but steadily, pouring your-selves out for each other in acts of love" (Ephesians 4:1-2 MSG).

The Mission of HighQuest

> **The HighQuest mission is to equip men to:**
> • Know Christ deeply
> • Reflect Christ authentically
> • Share Christ intentionally

Equipping Men

Equipping means "to prepare by training or instruction." It is different than teaching. While teaching is important, equipping is essential. While teaching provides information, equipping provides skills.

In order for men to follow Christ for a lifetime, they need to be trained to face the challenges that lie ahead in the journey. Learning and practicing core skill sets (or spiritual disciplines) are essential, if a man is to walk effectively and authentically with Christ over the course of his life.

Becoming equipped consists of acquiring the proper skills and tools in order to face an ever-changing landscape with confidence. A lack of proper training and equipment results in fear and frustration. Being properly equipped means having the right concepts, principles, tools, and skills to walk with a real God in a real world.

• Know Christ Deeply

Most men find their identity in their accomplishments, titles or positions. Our lives are spent trying to prove our competence while living in constant fear that we will someday be found out and exposed. But what if our lives were based not on **what** we did but on **who** we know? Jesus said in John 17:3, "Now this is eternal life: that they may know you, the only true God, and Jesus Christ, whom you have sent."

The Bible's perspective is that knowing Christ is both our greatest privilege and our greatest challenge. God has put within the heart of every man the desire to know Him. The desire may be masked by the callousness of indifference, the cloud of sin, or the compulsion of busyness, but it is there.

Paul fanned the spark by letting go of the fickle facade of status and achievement, to focus on knowing Christ.

"What is more, I consider everything a loss compared to the surpassing greatness of knowing Christ Jesus my Lord, for whose sake I have lost all things. I consider them rubbish, that I may gain Christ…I want to know Christ and the power of his resurrection and the fellowship of sharing in his sufferings, becoming like him in his death" (Philippians 3:8, 10).

Knowing Christ is the heart of our journey of faith. Everything flows from this one relationship which consists of more than believing facts about Christ. It is the personal, progressive process of walking with Christ through all of life's situations. Knowing Him demands honest and consistent communication with him through the shared experiences of normal everyday living.

Knowing Christ is the incredible privilege of a personal friendship with the living God. In John 15:5, Jesus told his disciples, "I no longer call you servants ...instead I have called you friends." Friendship with God is not a relationship of equals. It is, however, the awesome opportunity for children to relate to their heavenly Father. As we learn, believe, and obey the will of God, he reveals more of his heart to us through his Spirit.

• Reflect Christ Authentically

Historically church leaders have agreed that the primary purpose of our lives is to glorify God. But glorifying God is not in its essence, the common practice of singing worship songs or thinking mystical thoughts. We glorify God as we reflect his revealed nature through our everyday, ordinary lives.

"And we, who with unveiled faces all reflect the Lord's glory, are being transformed into his likeness with ever-increasing glory, which comes from the Lord, who is the Spirit" (2 Corinthians 3:18).

We reflect Christ as we are transformed in character, values, beliefs, and behavior. This inside-out transformation shapes our new identity in Christ and makes us authentic. We are becoming who we really are.

As the moon reflects the light (glory) of the sun, so we are to reflect the light (glory) of God. We, like the moon, are dependent on an external source for light. As we grow to know him and our lives change to conform to his image, we become lights to those around us. "You are the light of the world," Jesus said. God wants to display his nature to the world by transforming the lives of men of faith.

Reflecting Christ requires a partnership in which God's Spirit works in us as we cooperate with him. Our response to God's Word is one of faith and obedience. The result is we are transformed to be more and more like Christ. We value what he values. We make our ways his ways. We make his truth our beliefs.

• Share Christ Intentionally
God's plan is to reach people through people. We are like links in a chain. Each spiritual generation is a link to the next. Jesus said to His disciples during his final hours on earth,

"You did not choose me, but I chose you and appointed you to go and bear fruit—fruit that will last" (John 5:16).

He made a similar statement in Matthew 4:19 when he said, "Follow Me and I will make you fishers of men" (NASB).

Following Christ naturally leads to fishing for men. "Fishing for men" (spiritually investing in others) is our part in adding new links to the spiritual chain.

God's strategy for reaching people with the good news of his love is through people. When Jesus gathered his disciples together after the resurrection, he gave them this mission:

These few, ordinary men turned their world upside down.

They launched a world-changing movement without the aid of technology, political clout or social status. They did it one person at a time.

The Components of HighQuest

As you are going, make disciples! **Matthew 28:19**

Each HighQuest unit has two components: life skills and life issues. The life skills are developed around life issues.

• Life Skills

Each HighQuest unit helps develop core skills or disciplines that a man needs to walk with God for a lifetime. Each skill is an historical spiritual discipline that has been used by believers of all ages and cultures for the purpose of developing spiritual maturity.

In any area of life, skilled habits can make us more effective. Those who have developed the skill of a smooth golf swing have greater freedom on the golf course. Men who have developed the skill sets of an effective conditioning program have greater freedom to engage in various physical activities. A doctor who has developed surgery skills has greater freedom in the operating room. The skills themselves are not the goal but the means to something greater.

Spiritual habits are avenues of God's grace that allow us to tap into His power. They result in increased freedom to experience Christ. New skills, however, do require time and practice to become habits. At first they even seem mechanical and awkward, but with persistence, the new skills will become a natural part of your lifestyle. Then you will be free to focus on your relationship with Christ rather than the discipline.

Paul knew that spiritual disciplines were important. He told Timothy, "Do not waste time arguing over godless ideas and old wives' tales. Spend your time and energy in training yourself for spiritual fitness. Physical exercise has some value, but spiritual exercise is much more important, for it promises a reward in both this life and the next" (I Timothy 4:7-10 NLT). He also reminded the young believers in Corinth of his own commitment to discipline and why it was important to him.

"Do you not know that those who run in a race all run, but only one receives the prize? Run in such a way that you may win. And everyone who competes in the games exercises self-control in all things. They then do it to receive a perishable wreath, but we an imperishable. Therefore I run in such a way, as not without aim; I box in such a way, as not beating the air; but I buffet my body and make it my slave, lest possibly, after I have preached to others, I myself should be disqualified" (I Corinthians 9:24-27 NASB).

Spiritual training -- developing the habit of spiritual disciplines -- is absolutely necessary for our journey with Christ. The following life skills are developed in the HighQuest series:
> **HighQuest I**:   Meeting with God
> **HighQuest II**:   Gripping the Scripture
> **HighQuest III**: Investing your life

• Life Issues
Each HighQuest unit will look at a key life issue. These life issues are foundational concepts on which you will need to build your life. HighQuest will only give you an introduction to these important topics, but with the skills you learn, you can continue to explore and develop these and other life issues on your own or with a few other men in a HighQuest Forum.

It is important to realize that understanding and wisdom come as we depend on the Holy Spirit and dig into the Scripture as if looking for buried treasure. The Bible is not written as a text book or an encyclopedia. Topics are not neatly arranged and conveniently located. The Bible speaks to every issue we will face in life but in the context of the stories of real people; people who have traveled their own high quest.

The Scripture is both an autobiography of God as he reveals himself through history and a life application manual. God reveals principles and truths that teach us how to live life effectively. His principles are timeless. His truth is always true. The story line of the Bible is set in a particular culture at a particular time in history, but the teaching is ageless. Jesus said that, "Heaven and earth will pass away. But my words will never pass away" (Matthew 24:35).

Learning to go to the Bible for answers to life's questions is a mark of a disciple of Christ. Knowing that God has spoken and will speak to you is a mark of faith. As you search the Scripture, depend on the Holy Spirit as your guide and instructor. He will not just speak to your mind but to your heart as well.

HIGHQUEST

His Nature

SET UP SESSIONS

The focus of this Set Up Session is to get acquainted as a forum and understand what *HighQuest II: His Nature* is all about.

1. Begin by getting acquainted with the men in your forum. Each man should share his contact information on page 11 so the others can record it.

2. If this is a new group or there are new people in the group,:
   a. Each man should share his Personal Profile (pages 12-15) so others can learn and record it.
   b. Each man should fill out and share their Personal Time Line on page 21.

3. Review the material on a HighQuest Forum on pages 16-20. Emphasize that each week during your Forum, each person will be sharing from their AWG journal and their Check the Map.

4. Review the fundamentals of an AWG (page 22) along with how to fill out the Check the Map (page 23). A full explanation of an AWG is found in the Appendix (pages 144-148).

5. Read the introduction to His Nature (pages 24-26).

6. Review the material on Scripture memory (pages 27-30). Emphasize the need to review all verses daily not just the new ones. Build the memory and review into your daily schedule.

7. Review Planned Meditation on pages 31-37. The weekly format is the same as in *HighQuest II: His Image.* Your meditation form is on day 5 of each week and is over the Scripture memory verse for the topic. You will do part A of the meditation the first week and part B the second week.

If this is the first unit the men have done of *HighQuest II: Reflecting Christ Authentically,* you will need to walk through a sample meditation form on pages 140-143 in the Appendix.

SET UP SESSION

Name

Address

Phone   **Email**

Name

Address

Phone   **Email**

Name

Address

Phone   **Email**

Name

Address

Phone   **Email**

Name

Address

Phone   **Email**

PERSONAL PROFILE

NAME

Family
_____
_____
_____
_____

Birth date   Anniversary
_____

Places lived
_____

Skills/hobbies
_____
_____
_____

Job history
_____
_____
_____
_____
_____
_____
_____

First car
_____

Nickname
_____
_____

NAME

Family

Birth date   Anniversary

Places lived

Skills/hobbies

Job history

First car

Nickname

PERSONAL PROFILE

NAME	

Family
_____
_____
_____
_____
_____

Birth date _____ Anniversary _____

Places lived
_____
_____

Skills/hobbies
_____
_____
_____

Job history
_____
_____
_____
_____
_____
_____
_____
_____

First car
_____

Nickname
_____
_____

14

NAME	

Family

Birth date   Anniversary

Places lived

Skills/hobbies

Job history

First car

Nickname

Forum Essentials

The HighQuest forum is an environment in which 3-4 men meet for perspective, encouragement, and accountability.

In order to deal with these issues, the HighQuest Forum cre-

> **Most men tend to live lives that are:**
> - *isolated rather than connected*
> - *compartmentalized rather than integrated*
> - *disengaged rather than engaged*

ates a consistent place where men can be listened to, taken seriously, and understood.

There are four essentials of a HighQuest Forum: Connection, Exploration, Application, and Intercession. Each one is a vital part of the Forum experience.

• Connection

> The operative question for the beginning of each HQ Forum is ***"Because we care, what do we need to know?"***

Most men are asking the question, "Who knows and who cares?" The HighQuest Forum creates a safe environment in which men can relate with one another on a deeper level than news, weather, and sports. It is safe because each man is given the opportunity to honestly discuss real and relevant issues in his life and still be accepted and respected by the other men. It is also safe because nothing is shared outside the HighQuest Forum without permission.

There are additional reasons why the HighQuest Forum is ideal for 3-4 men.
1. It allows time for everyone to participate in a 60-90 minute format.
2. It gives greater flexibility for meeting locations: home, office, or restaurant.

• Exploration

> The operative question is *"Because God's Word is true, what are you discovering?"*

Every man needs to learn how to feed himself from the Word of God. Passivity is devastating for men on a quest with God. Most men learn best when they are involved in the process of discovery. Passively listening to the truth of God's Word as it is taught by others, is like a man in a canoe with no paddle. His ability to navigate the river is extremely limited. But when you give him the skills to discover truth for himself, you equip him to travel the waterways of truth for the rest of his life.

Most men lack confidence to personally go to the Bible and gain insight for their lives. In HighQuest men develop the skills needed to explore and gain understanding from God's Word. In addition, the HighQuest Forum gives an opportunity to share personal insights as well as learn from others.

• Application

> The operative question is *"Because God's Word is relevant, what is He telling you to do?"*

In order to follow Christ on this journey, men need more than insight. They need application. Application takes the truths of the Bible and integrates them into the fabric of life. We mature as we apply God's truth to our personal, family, and professional life.

Spiritual truth must not be isolated to a spiritual compartment of life while most of our thoughts and energy go into the business of everyday living. God's plan is to integrate his truth into our everyday, ordinary lives. There is no isolated spiritual compartment -- just spiritual men living real life in a real world.

The HighQuest Forum is an environment where men are loved and accepted yet challenged to change. Men need a "band of brothers" who will stand up for them and to them: men who will challenge them to do what is right and celebrate when they do it.

• **Intercession**

The operative question is *"Because God cares, how can we support you in prayer?"*

The HighQuest Forum includes personal prayer for and with each other. Holding up each other in prayer is a critical force for encouragement and power. Sharing needs and victories together in the context of prayer, builds a connection and puts the focus on God's work in our lives.

Praying together is often the most difficult part of the High-Quest Forum. It is important not only for men to pray for each other during the week but also during the HighQuest Forum. Not everyone will be comfortable praying in a group. The leader will need to be flexible and responsive to the backgrounds of the members. However, as the group develops a greater level of honesty and transparency, prayer usually becomes a less formal and more relaxed part of the HighQuest Forum experience.

Using a conversational style of prayer allows member to participate at their own comfort level. The leader will need to guard this prayer time as it can easily become absorbed by the other parts of the HighQuest Forum.

SET UP SESSION

Forum Format

A forum is like a rope that is woven together from separate strands. Each component is a strand that gives strength to the whole. It is important that you use the whole rope during each forum. A forum will not be effective if strands are missing. The forum facilitator will need to govern when to move to the next component.

The best way to keep moving is simply to ask the next operative question. Avoid letting one part dominate. This doesn't mean you have to spend the same amount of time on each question. For example, some weeks critical issues raised in the group may cause you to spend more time on intercession. Allow the Holy Spirit freedom to lead the group but maintain cohesion and direction.

A typical HighQuest Forum meets for 60 minutes. The hour can be divided into the following strands:
(If you have 90 minutes, simply expand each strand by 50%)

- **Connection:** 15 minutes
- **Exploration:** 25 minutes
- **Application:** 10 minutes
- **Intercession:** 10 minutes

Forum Ground Rules

It is important to establish some simple yet critical guidelines for your forum. These basic ground rules will create the security and trust that men need if they are to become honest, vulnerable, and transparent.

- I will commit to the group; make attendance to the weekly Forum a priority.
- I will be willing to be transparent and encourage other

members of the group to do likewise.

• I will complete the assignment for the week and be ready to share with the group.

• I will hold (in confidence) the personal matters shared in the group.

Signed: _____

Forum Discussion Notes

As you meet each week in your HighQuest Forum, you will be covering: Connection, Exploration, Application and Intercession.

At the end of each weekly journaling session, there is a page for taking notes during your forum. This page allows you to record thoughts and ideas that others share during the discussion.

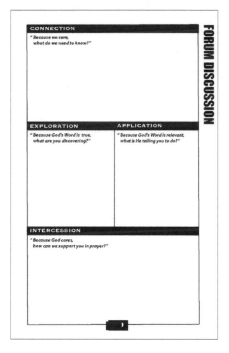

Personal Journey Timeline
(Note significant events that tell your story)

Birth

Present

+

−

APPOINTMENT WITH GOD (AWG) REVIEW

In HighQuest I: Knowing Christ Deeply, you learned how to have an AWG using the outline of Read, Record, Reflect, and Respond. You will continue to use that format in this unit of HighQuest.

Developing the life skill of meeting with God on a regular (preferably daily) basis takes effort and time. We do not learn new habits quickly. But once we learn them, they allow us to focus on the result more than the process. We hope your AWG will become a lifelong habit on your quest with Christ. As you gain greater skill in the use of the AWG, you will gain greater freedom to modify it and make it fit your personality and life style without losing the essential ingredients.

In this unit of HighQuest, you will not be taught how to have an AWG, but you will be given the opportunity to reinforce what you have already learned and become more consistent. If you have not developed the life skill of an AWG, we suggest you refer to one of the units in HighQuest I before continuing with this unit.

Remember, the given passages are not to limit you but to start you. You may read more or less than suggested. The AWG is designed to allow you to listen to and dialogue with God. As you read and God speaks through his Word, stop and listen. Your AWG is to help you connect with Christ on a regular and personal basis; to sit at his feet and listen to his words.

By now the mechanics of an AWG should be fading into the background allowing you to focus on your time in Christ's presence. The key to meeting God in His Word is to ask three core questions: What does it say? What does it mean? How can I apply it? The AWG format in HighQuest was designed to help you think that way.

Check the Map

HighQuest I is laid out in a six-day sequence with journal pages for five days and a sixth day to "check the map." A map gives us a picture of where we have been, where we are today, and where we are headed. In the same way, the Check the Map page is a time to review the past week and highlight what God has been teaching you.

A suggested way to review is to take key ideas from the week and list them on the Check the Map page. Once you have all ideas written down, summarize by stating the central theme or big idea. You may also review by focusing on one specific day that stood out to you. Write down summary thoughts from that day looking for one big idea that brings focus to the week.

God speaks to us through the Scripture in a variety of ways. You will notice an acronym on the Check the Map page that will guide your review and application. These questions will help you put into practice what God is saying.

As you listen to God speak through his Word during the past week, is there a ….

> **S** in to avoid?
> **P** romise to claim?
> **E** xample to follow?
> **C** ommand to obey?
> **K** nowledge about God to believe?

You do not need to answer all of these questions each week but simply use them as a way to listen to God. When something stands out, act on it!

Writing out an application is a way to move from the conceptual to the practical. Make your application a way to act on what you have heard God say. Make it **specific, short term** and **measurable.** Remember, the most profound application is often a very simple one.

You will use the Check the Map page in your HighQuest Forum for the "Exploration" time.

LIFE ISSUE: His Nature

Following Jesus is more than a "get out of jail free" card. When Jesus invites people to follow him, he has more in mind than "redemption" (as important as that is). His goal is not to make people comfortable, give them a better set of rules, or make them successful. His goal in inviting people to follow him, is to transform their lives to look like his own.

"A student is not above his teacher, but everyone who is fully trained will be like his teacher" (Luke 6:40).

This transformation is more than a behavioral makeover. Jesus is not interested in outward, moral cosmetics. His goal is to change people deep in their hearts to reflect his very nature. The apostle Peter expands this concept as he begins his second letter to the early believers.

"Through these he has given us his very great and precious promises, so that through them you may participate in the divine nature and escape the corruption in the world caused by evil desires" (2 Peter 1:4).

Reflecting Christ's divine nature is at the heart of following Christ. It may not always be our goal, but it is his. We may be satisfied with a little religion, a touch of respectability, a dose of Bible knowledge or even Christian friends. But this is not the true Christian life, nor God's purpose. In Romans 8:28, Paul gives us the assurance that "God works for the good of those who love him, who have been called according to his purpose." He then defines God's purpose:

"For those God foreknew he also predestined to be conformed to the likeness of his Son, that he might be the firstborn among many brothers" (Romans 8:29).

God's purpose and our good are wrapped up in becoming conformed to his likeness. Stop now and read 2 Peter 1:3-11.

In this passage Peter expands Paul's theme of what it means to be "conformed to the likeness of his Son." This passage is the foundation for this unit of *HighQuest II: His Nature.*

God did not leave us guessing as to what he meant regarding his nature. Obviously, God reserves some of his qualities for himself alone. But there are qualities he desires to share with people of faith who are part of his family. Peter lists some qualities we are to reflect:

"For this very reason, make every effort to add to your faith goodness; and to goodness, knowledge; and to knowledge, self-control; and to self-control, perseverance; and to perseverance, godliness; and to godliness, brotherly kindness; and to brotherly kindness, love" (2 Peter 1:5-7).

These traits could be paraphrased as:
- Moral excellence
- True knowledge
- Self control
- Hopeful persistence
- Reverent wonder
- Genuine love

In this unit of HighQuest, you will explore these six traits in more depth. You will spend two weeks on each trait using the personal skills of AWG, Scripture memory, and planned meditation. In your AWGs, you memorize and meditate on a key verse for the trait as well as reflect on passages that serve as cross-references.

When Peter said "add to your faith" he means comprehensively, not sequentially. The composite, not the order, is important. God calls us to acquire and develop all of them all the time. Peter said the benefit comes as they are yours "and increasing." We develop these Christ-like qualities over our entire lifetime, and we are to give them our constant attention.

LIFE ISSUE: His Nature

These qualities are not optional. They are not a series of electives. They serve as an integral part of our journey of maturity and fruitfulness in Christ. Peter explains why they are so important. They are critical for life and godliness (v. 3), knowing Christ (v. 8), perspective and victory (v. 9), verifying our calling (v. 10), and investing in eternity (v. 11).

Reflecting Christ authentically (his nature) is linked critically both to knowing Christ and sharing Christ. Each supports and builds on the other. As we reflect more of Christ's nature, we grow deeper in our relationship with him. As we grow deeper in our relationship with him, we reflect more of his nature. Likewise, our passion and skill in sharing Christ is linked to our reflecting and knowing him. Together, these three core aspects of our faith journey are like a tripod. We can't develop one without the others.

Peter tells us that these traits are not automatic. Rather, Peter calls us to "make every effort" to add to the foundation of our faith urgently, intentionally, diligently, and continually as opposed to casually, passively, reluctantly, or periodically.

However, this cannot be done on our own power. Thankfully, God, through his Holy Spirit, gives us all we need in order to achieve his purpose of being conformed to his likeness:

"His divine power has given us everything we need for life and godliness through our knowledge of him who called us by his own glory and goodness" (2 Peter 1:3).

God did not set us up to fail. He gives his Holy Spirit to each believer and calls us to be filled with and walk in that Spirit (Ephesians 5:18). God simply calls us to tap into the power he already has given us. Then armed with his Spirit and his promises we walk in faith. Now let's roll up our sleeves and get to work.

As you explore reflecting *His Nature* in the weeks ahead, remember that his resources are available not only to give you understanding but to transform you from the inside out. Ask God to work deep in your heart as well as your mind.

Gripping the Scripture

Mountain climbing requires the skill of attaching secure points in the snow or rock along the route to serve as anchors. Pitons are wedged in the cracks of rocks and ice screws are used in snow. Carabineers are then attached to these anchors giving the climber a secure point to attach his rope. Solid points of attachment are critical for a safe and successful climb.

Setting anchor points in Scripture is also necessary for a successful journey with Christ. In HighQuest II, we will be teaching you how to get a grip on the Scripture so you can firmly attach yourself to God's truth as an anchor along your journey. Getting a grip on Scripture requires the combination of memory and meditation.

In an age of Palm Pilots and computers and myriad Bible translations, Scripture memory has become a lost art. In the days before the printing press, few people had access to written material. Only the educated elite would own or access books. Memorizing was practiced as much for necessity as for its inherent value.

In HighQuest II, we have selected the verses for you. Each verse is seminal for the given topic. Later, you will need to identify and select your own based on the issues you are facing in life. As you spend time in the Word and face life issues, God will highlight a verse to reflect on. Use what you learn in HighQuest II to get a grip on the Word and anchor yourself to the truth.

As you experience the value of **memorizing** Scripture and combine it with the habit of planned **meditation**, you will have a skill set that equips you for the life long journey.

• Memorizing

You may be thinking, "So why memorize Scripture today when I can pull it up on my Palm Pilot in a matter of seconds?" The answer lies not so much in the head but in the heart. It is not so much a question of how much of the Scripture do we have but rather how much does the Scripture have of us?

Scripture memory secures the Word of God deep into our hearts where the Holy Spirit can use it to pull us up to new

27

heights. Memorizing Scripture lends stability to our lives on treacherous terrain and slippery slopes. Possessing the skill of using it can be the difference between a serious fall and a successful climb.

You may have memorized Scripture in the past for a variety of external reasons that have not held up in your adult world. Memorizing Scripture is often treated as a kid's thing that is not relevant for adults. But when you discover how to grip God's word through the combination of memorization and meditation, you will find one of the most powerful skills for life transformation.

The Bible gives us some practical reasons why we should memorize Scripture or "hide it in our hearts" as was the Old Testament expression. As you learn the skill of Scripture memory and begin to enjoy its benefits, you will discover that each of these benefits will touch your life at some time. Here are a few to consider.

Memorization Benefits

1. Victory over sin: Psalm 119:11
I have hidden your word in my heart, that I might not sin against you.
2. Think correctly: Philippians 4:8
And now, dear brothers and sisters, let me say one more thing as I close this letter. Fix your thoughts on what is true and honorable and right. Think about things that are pure and lovely and admirable. Think about things that are excellent and worthy of praise.
3. Worship: Psalm 119:164
I will praise you seven times a day because all your laws are just.
4. Guidance: Psalms 119:24
Your decrees please me; they give me wise advice.
5. Prayer: John 15:7
But if you stay joined to me and my words remain in you, you may ask any request you like, and it will be granted!
6. Counseling: Isaiah 50:4

The Sovereign Lord has given me his words of wisdom, so that I know what to say to all these weary ones. Morning by morning he wakens me and opens my understanding to his will.

Memorization Principles

Look over the following suggestions for effective Scripture memory. Regardless of your natural ability to memorize, you may be able to get a verse into your short term memory in a matter of a few minutes. However, it takes regular practice and review to retain it.

1. Select a good translation to memorize from (NIV, NKJ, NASB, etc).
2. Before you start to memorize a verse, read it aloud several times.
3. Write out the verse on a small card so you can carry it with you. (In HighQuest II, the verses are printed in the back of the book.)
4. Learn the topic, reference, and first phrase as a unit. Memorize the verse word for word.
5. Repeat #4 and add a phrase at a time until you have the entire verse. Always quote the reference before and after you quote the verse.
6. Repeat the verse out loud several times a day.
7. Keep the verse with you and review it 4-5 times as you go through the day.
8. Quote the verse to someone who will listen.
9. Review each verse at least once a day for 7 weeks.

The most critical element in Scripture memory is review, review, review! The most important time to review a verse repeatedly is right after you can quote the whole verse from memory (topic, reference, verse, reference) without making a mistake. Review the verse at least once a day, preferably several times each day. The more you review, the greater the retention.

Thorough learning is an important concept. A verse should not be considered memorized when you can quote it accurately. Only when you have reviewed it every day for 7 weeks will it be ingrained in your memory.

In HighQuest II: *His Nature,* you will memorize 6 verses. As you memorize a new verse, you will need to review the old ones as well. The goal is that at the end of this unit, you will be able to quote all 6 verses word perfect at one time. For a list of verses you will be memorizing, go to the chart on pages 38 and 39.

Meditation

"'Meditation is simply thought prolonged and directed to a single object. Our mystic chambers where thoughts abide are the secret workshop of an unseen Sculptor chiseling living forms for a deathless future. Personality and influences are modeled here. Hence, the Biblical injunction 'Keep your heart with all diligence, for out of it are the issues of life.'

A. T. Pierson

Meditation is chewing. It is like the graphic picture of a cow and her process of mastication. It involves bringing up previously digested food for renewed grinding and its preparation for assimilation. Meditation is pondering and viewing various thoughts by mulling them over in the mind and heart. It is the processing of mental food. We might call it "thought digestion." "Chewing" upon a thought deliberately and thoroughly, thus providing a vital link between theory and action. What metabolism is to the physical body of the cow, meditation is to your mental and spiritual life.

Meditation is analyzing. It is the art of taking a good, long look at a given object as the craftsman does his dazzling jewel...polishing the diamond to reflect all its light and beauty. Meditation on a portion of the Holy Bible is like gazing at a prism of many facets, turning the stones from angle to angle in the bright sunlight. Steady and constant reflection reveals unlimited beauties from the Scriptures which will never otherwise be seen. "Open my eyes to see the wonderful truths in your law" (Psalms 119:18 NLT).

Meditation is action. Someone has described it: "Making words into thoughts and thoughts into actions." It is mentally planning ahead with definite action in mind for accomplishing a job.

"Muse" was the name given to an ancient Greek god who spent much time in solitude and thinking. The statue of "The Thinker" is the artistic concept of deep concentration and absorption. Add an "a" to the beginning of "muse" and you have: "amuse—sports, games, television and a score of other tools used by the enemy to keep God's men from concentrating on man's God.

Beware of getting alone with your own thoughts. Get alone

31

LIFE SKILL: Planned Meditation

with God's thoughts. There is danger in rummaging through waste and barren desert thoughts that can be labeled—day dreaming or worse. Don't meditate upon yourself but dwell upon Him—seek God in your inner thought life. There is always danger in meditating upon our problems. Develop the habit of reflecting upon the Word of God and therein find the answers to your problems."[1]

"You satisfy me more than the richest of foods. I will praise you with songs of joy. I lie awake thinking of you, meditating on you through the night" (Psalm 63:5-6 NLT).

Planned Meditation

In HighQuest II, we will be using Planned Meditation (PM). This form of meditation includes four specific steps that will guide the meditation process in an inductive manner. Thinking inductively involves taking things apart before putting them back together into a conclusion. Deductive thinking starts with the conclusion and works back to the parts. The inductive form of meditation starts by asking "What does it say?" followed by "What does it mean", and concluding with "How can I apply it?"

When meditation is added to the skill of Scripture memory, God's Word becomes more than knowledge. It allows the Spirit to access the deepest part of our soul and results in transformed lives. The writer of Hebrews said,

"For the word of God is full of living power. It is sharper than the sharpest knife, cutting deep into our innermost thoughts and desires. It exposes us for what we really are. Nothing in all creation can hide from him. Everything is naked and exposed before his eyes. This is the God to whom we must explain all that we have done" (Hebrews 4:12-13 NLT).

An important principle of meditating on Scripture is to understand the context of the verse in question. The context is the

1 A Primer on Meditation, The Navigators

setting in which a statement (or verse) is made. Often we mis-interpret a verse because we fail to understand the context. The context is found by looking at what is said before and after the verse on which you are meditating. This may involve reading a paragraph or even a chapter. In this unit of High-Quest II, we have designed your AWG passages to incorporate the context of the verse you are memorizing.

Another principle of meditation is to "interpret Scripture by Scripture." This means looking at other parts of the Bible to add insight and understanding. This part of meditation is called "cross referencing". The more time you spend in the Bible, the easier it will be to find cross references. Some Bibles have a cross reference list in the page margin or in an index at the back. Cross references may be on a word, concept or idea.

This HighQuest unit has passages for your AWG that are cross references for the verse you are memorizing. Some of these passages are examples; others amplify the words or ideas in the verse you are memorizing.

Although the passages selected for your AWG are tied to a theme, don't worry if you don't always make the connection. Remember that your AWG is an opportunity to listen to God. Listen first and connect what you hear to the selected theme second.

Planned Meditation Steps (see sample page 36-37).
1. Writing the verse
Begin your planned meditation by writing out the verse (from memory if you can). You can use this step to check your memory and it will serve as a visible reference later.

2. Defining key words
Identify each significant word in the verse. Using a diction-ary, write down all relevant definitions for each word. A dictionary can expand our normal understanding of a word and lead to new insight. Try reading the verse using a word definition or synonym.

If you have access to a Biblical dictionary like the Vines New Testament Word Study, you can also find some additional

33

LIFE SKILL: Planned Meditation

insight into word meanings.

3. Saying it again

Write out the verse in your own words. Use what you have discovered from the definitions above to say it differently yet not losing any of the meaning. This could be called your paraphrase.

4. Breaking it down

Now you should reflect on the verse for greater understanding. You have been looking at what it says, now look for what it means. One way to meditate to gain understanding is to ask questions. Questions can help us see new patterns and relationships.

• **See:** Make observations as to what is being said. Look for the main ideas or concepts. Look for the connections between thoughts and ideas. Be an explorer or detective. The more you look, the more you will see.

• **Search:** Look for answers to the questions: Who? What? Where? Why? How? Some of these questions will be answered in the verse itself, others may be implied. Look for additional insight from some of the passages you used in your AWG to answer your questions. Be bold in asking questions even if you don't come up with answers.

• **So what:** The "so what?" question helps you turn knowledge into practice. It keeps you from remaining theoretical. You want to think in terms of how Scripture can relate to real life. It involves asking an if/then question such as, "If what I have observed is true, what difference would/should it make? How could it relate to my family, neighborhood, marketplace or personal life? "

Try expressing it this way, "If _____

34

(state the truth), then _____(state the implication).

There are always a number of implications for any discovered truth. Some may be relevant to where you are and others may be relevant later.

5. Finding the bottom line

Write a statement that summarizes what you think is the main principle or idea of the verse. This is an objective state-ment which answers the question "What is this verse saying?" or "Why did God include this verse in Scripture?"

6. Putting it into Action

You will apply this verse to your life using the "Check the Map" page in your AWG section. This step involves identifying the key truth God is impressing on your heart and then look-ing for a way to put that truth into action.

SET UP SESSION

Write it out *(Copy it from your Bible)*

"I am the vine; you are the branches. If a man remains in me and I in him, he will bear much fruit; apart from me you can do nothing."

Define key words *(Use a dictionary)*

VINE: (grapevine): A plant with a woody stem that bears grapes

BRANCH: Any woody extension growing from a trunk: any part or extension of a main body

REMAIN: To be left when the rest has been taken way; to stay in the same place; to continue, go on being; endure, persist.

FRUIT: Product: a plant product: the result, consequence or product of any action.

NOTHING: nonexistence; insignificance or non important; vain useless; of little or no value, trivial

Say it again *(Put it in your own words)*

Jesus says, "I am the trunk and you are the branches. If you stay connected to Me, you will be fruitful. Without My life giving resources, you will dry up and be useless."

Write it out *(Copy it from your Bible)*

> *"I am the vine; you're the branches. If a man remains in me and I in him, he will bear much fruit; apart from me you can do nothing."*

Break it down *(See, Search & So What?)*

> *Jesus is clarifying the relationship I have with Him. I am dependent on the vine for nourishment. The vine is the source, support and anchor for the branches. Fruit is not automatic. The "if" word makes it conditional. The condition is my choice to remain in the vine. There is freedom to disconnect but the results will be fruitlessness.*
>
> *Remaining in or continuing in means to persevere... not just temporary or periodically. What is the "fruit"? It could be the character of Christ i.e. fruit of the Holy Spirit or it could be good works or deeds. Jesus gives the results of remaining and not remaining. Failing to remain in Him results in activity but stuff of little value or importance. It's not that we can't do something but that it amounts to nothing of any real value.*

Find the bottom line *(The main principle)*

> *God's plan is to produce fruit through me. He is a ready source of divine poser but I must choose to remain vitally connected to him. I can live without this union with Him but it will result in activity without significance. motion without meaning.*

37

SET UP SESSION

Session	Topic/AWG Passages	Memory
Week 1	Moral Excellence (A)	1 Peter 2:9
Day 1	2 Peter 1:3-11	
Day 2	1 Peter 2:4-12	
Day 3	Philippians 4:1-9	
Day 4	Matthew 7:1-12	
Day 5	Planned Meditation Part 1 (1 Peter 2:9)	
Day 6	Check the Map	
Week 2	Moral Excellence (B)	Review 1 Peter 2:9
Day 1	Hebrews 11:23-29	
Day 2	Daniel 3:1-28	
Day 3	Acts 4:1-21	
Day 4	Matthew 4:1-11	
Day 5	Planned Meditation Part 2 (1 Peter 2:9)	
Day 6	Check the Map	
Week 3	True Knowledge (A)	Colossians 1:9
Day 1	Colossians 1:4-12	
Day 2	1 John 4:1-8	
Day 3	John 13:1-12	
Day 4	Matthew 13:1-12	
Day 5	Planned Meditation Part 1 (Colossians 1:9)	
Day 6	Check the Map	
Week 4	True Knowledge (B)	Review Colossians 1:9
Day 1	Hosea 6:1-11	
Day 2	Ephesians 1:15-23	
Day 3	Proverbs 8:1-13	
Day 4	Luke 2:40-52	
Day 5	Planned Meditation Part 2 (Colossians 1:9)	
Day 6	Check the Map	
Week 5	Self Control (A)	2 Timothy 1:7
Day 1	2 Timothy 1:1-11	
Day 2	Acts 24:10-26	
Day 3	Galatians 5:16-26	
Day 4	1 Corinthians 9:16-27	
Day 5	Planned Meditation Part 1 (2 Timothy 1:7)	
Day 6	Check the Map	
Week 6	Self Control (B)	Review 2 Timothy 1:7
Day 1	Romans 6:4-14	
Day 2	Proverbs 25:28; 6:4-11	
Day 3	Matthew 26:36-54	
Day 4	Ecclesiastes 3:1-10	
Day 5	Planned Meditation Part 2 (2 Timothy 1:7)	
Day 6	Check the Map	

Session	Topic/AWG Passages	Memory
Week 7	Hopeful Perseverance (A)	Hebrews 12:1
Day 1	Hebrews 12:1-11	
Day 2	Luke 8:4-15	
Day 3	James 1:1-8	
Day 4	Romans 5:1-5	
Day 5	Planned Meditation Part 1 (Hebrews 12:1)	
Day 6	Check the Map	
Week 8	Hopeful Perseverance (B)	Review Hebrews 12:1
Day 1	1 Peter 2:18-25	
Day 2	1 Corinthians 15:50-58	
Day 3	Revelation 2:1-7	
Day 4	1 Thessalonians 1:1-10	
Day 5	Planned Meditation Part 2 (Hebrews 12:1)	
Day 6	Check the Map	
Week 9	Reverent Wonder (A)	1 Timothy 4:7-8
Day 1	1 Timothy 4:6-10	
Day 2	1 Timothy 6:1-11	
Day 3	2 Timothy 3:1-12	
Day 4	John 17:4-12	
Day 5	Planned Meditation Part 1 (1 Timothy 4:7-8)	
Day 6	Check the Map	
Week 10	Reverent Wonder (B)	Review 1 Timothy 4:7-8
Day 1	Psalm 33:1-18	
Day 2	Deuteronomy 10:12-22	
Day 3	Proverbs 1:7; 3:7; 8:13; 14:26-7; 16:6; 19:23; 22:4; 23:17	
Day 4	Acts 9:19-31	
Day 5	Planned Meditation Part 2 (1 Timothy 4:7-8)	
Day 6	Check the Map	
Week 11	Genuine Love (A)	1 Peter 1:22
Day 1	1 Peter 1:17-25	
Day 2	Romans 12:9-21	
Day 3	1 Thessalonians 4:1-12	
Day 4	John 21:15-22	
Day 5	Planned Meditation Part 1 (1 Peter 1:22)	
Day 6	Check the Map	
Week 12	Genuine Love (B)	Review 1 Peter 1:22
Day 1	John 14:15-24	
Day 2	John 13:12-17; 31-35	
Day 3	Acts 2:32-47	
Day 4	1 John 2:1-11	
Day 5	Planned Meditation Part 2 (1 Peter 1:22)	
Day 6	Check the Map	

HIGHQUEST
His Nature

APPOINTMENT WITH GOD

The first trait of Christ's nature that Peter urges us to intentionally develop, is moral excellence: also called goodness, good character, praises or virtue in various translations. The Greek word comes from the root word for manliness or valor. "For this very reason, make every effort to add to your faith goodness (moral excellence)" (2 Peter 1:5).

Every culture has a set of norms or ideals that identifies with moral excellence. For some of our American history, those norms were derived from a biblical worldview. But today, morality is based on a subjective, fluctuating scale, valuing convenience, the feeling of the moment, and popular opinion as opposed to God's timeless nature and his word. As our culture drifts from a biblical worldview, it is imperative that we base morality on God and his unchanging word. Sadly, proclaiming believers align themselves more with the culture's view of morality than with Christ's.

We cannot manufacture moral excellence by ourselves. Rather, it becomes evident as we discover the reality of Christ's nature within us. Moral excellence displays the authenticity of the Christ follower. It is not an activity; it is an identity. When moral excellence defines a man's identity, that man's conduct, behavior and attitudes consistently reflect Christ's nature. People notice and can count on it. He is not one person at church and another at work. He doesn't talk one way and live another.

Moral excellence must be learned and practiced. We are not born with this. Our homes and churches must model, teach, expect, and celebrate moral excellence. Every man needs a band of brothers to hold him accountable for his moral excellence, support him when he fails, and celebrate when he succeeds.

The key verse for this session is 1 Peter 2:9. "But you are a chosen people, a royal priesthood, a holy nation, a people belonging to God, that you may declare the praises of him who called you out of darkness into his wonderful light" (NIV). The word "praises" is the same word found in 2 Peter1:5 (goodness or moral excellence) and translated as "excellencies" in other translations.

2 Peter 1: 5, 6

In view of this make every effort to respond to God's promises. Supplement your faith with a generous provision of moral excellence, ... knowledge, self control ... patience endurance ... godliness ... brotherly affection ... love

💭 — Add to your faith ....

1. Sanctification is progressive
2.   "   can be supplemented
   faith can be added to
3. Sanctification requires all the qualities of
4. Sanctification a shortage can be determental

✉️ ─

RECORD

You are a chosen people. You are a royal priests; a holy nation. God's very own possession.

REFLECT

You are special

Society   Child of God

RESPOND

READ

RECORD

Phil 4: 8

Fix your thought on what is
true, and honorable, and right, and pure,
and lovely, and admirable. Think
about things that are excellent and
worthy of praise. Keep putting into
practice all you have learned.

REFLECT

💭 Be careful what you think.

RESPOND

✉

Matthew 7:1-12

PLANNED MEDITATION

Write it out (Copy it from your Bible)

Define key words (Use a dictionary. Page 33)

Say it again (Put it in your own words. Page 34)

_____
_____
_____
_____
_____
_____
_____
_____
_____
_____
_____
_____
_____
_____
_____
_____
_____
_____
_____
_____
_____

LIFE APPLICATION _____
_____
_____
_____
_____

Is there a.....
S in to avoid?
P romise to claim?
E xample to follow?
C ommand to obey?
K nowledge to believe

48

CONNECTION

"Because we care, what do we need to know?"

EXPLORATION

"Because God's Word is true, what are you discovering?"

APPLICATION

"Because God's Word is relevant, what is He telling you to do?"

INTERCESSION

"Because God cares, how can we support you in prayer?"

The Greek word for moral excellence includes the concepts of strength, bravery, courage, and goodness. The first century valued moral excellence even outside the religious context. Moral excellence, then, implies courage; courage that remains constant in the face of opposition or an apathetic culture.

Moral excellence doesn't expect tranquility. Joseph, as a slave in Egypt, was just trying to do a good job. He had risen to favored status in the household of Potiphar but unfortunately, also caught the attention of Potiphar's promiscuous wife. Joseph displayed moral excellence as he consistently rebuffed her sexual advances. Falsely accused of rape, Joseph was spared death but not prison. No defense. No appeal. No hope.

Moral excellence means doing what is right even when it is not required, comfortable or known by others. One day as my young son and I were loading the car with our recent purchases, I realized the clerk failed to charge us for one of our items. It was an opportunity to teach honesty. I pointed out the mistake to my son and we went back and told the clerk. As we drove off, however, I was challenged as I reflected on the question, "Would I have corrected the bill if I had been alone?" Moral excellence means not compromising even if no one is looking. The United Stated Military Academy (West Point) calls it "the harder right," and it serves as a cornerstone of leadership.

Moral excellence is expensive. It may cost friendships, professional advancement, or even your job. Others may avoid, ridicule, or even attack you as you live out moral excellence. Compromise constantly threatens moral excellence at home and in the marketplace.

The Bible records the outcome of many whose lives reflected moral excellence. Most often, taking the moral high road invited or increased pain and suffering. They were not lured by comfort, pleasure or popularity. They resolved to follow God's ways regardless of the worldly outcome. Are you willing to be so bold? Do you have the courage to stand against our culture and be a man of moral excellence?

Heb. 11:24

"It was by faith Moses, when he grew up, refused to be called the son of Pharoah's daughter. He chose to share the oppression of God's people, instead of enjoying the fleeting pleasure of sin."

Moses was a poor slave son who won a position in the wealthest ruler in the world. A poor boy to rich boy. But by faith he saw the vacancy of wealth and gave it up to be a part of the suffering of God's people. He sought to redeem or rescue his people but in his own efforts he was a failure.

READ / RECORD

Shadrach, Meshach and Abednego replied, O Nebuchadnezzar, we do not need to defend ourselves. If we are thrown into the flaming furnace, the God whom we serve is able to save us. But if he doesn't we will never serve your gods

REFLECT

God is able to do all we ask or think. He is omnipotent. Nothing is impossible with God. He is able but will not go against his nature. He is a loving God who is always just, loving, working toward our best of needs.

Acts 4:12 There is salvation in no
other name! God has given no
other name under heaven by wich
we must be saved."
Acts 4:19

The high priest + family. arrested
Peter & John for teaching and
healing in the name of Jesus
Peter responds that there is power
in the name of Jesus. The
leaders realizing they had performed
a high miracle told the
disciples to stop their teaching
about Jesus and set Peter & John
free.

Matthew 4:1-11

Write it out *(Copy it from your Bible)*

Break it down *(See, Search & So What? Page 34)*

Find the bottom line *(The main principle. Page 35)*

SUMMARIZE KEY IDEAS

LIFE APPLICATION _____

Is there a.....
S in to avoid?
P romise to claim?
E xample to follow?
C ommand to obey?
K nowledge to believe

56

CONNECTION

"Because we care, what do we need to know?"

EXPLORATION

"Because God's Word is true, what are you discovering?"

APPLICATION

"Because God's Word is relevant, what is He telling you to do?"

INTERCESSION

"Because God cares, how can we support you in prayer?"

The second trait Peter highlights is "knowledge" or "spiritual understanding." This true knowledge is rooted in our relationship with Christ and linked to our understanding of his nature. "Seeing that His divine power has granted to us everything pertaining to life and godliness, through the true knowledge of Him who called us by His own glory and excellence" (2Peter 1:3). This kind of knowledge is more than correct doctrine. It comes out of our relationship with him.

True knowledge is more than we can acquire on our own. It requires a work of the Holy Spirit to open our hearts and minds to his truth. The necessity for this divine work compelled Paul to pray for the Colossian believers. If we are to be filled with the knowledge of his will, to have spiritual wisdom, to have spiritual understanding, we need the supernatural touch of his Holy Spirit.

"For this reason also, since the day we heard of it, we have not ceased to pray for you and to ask that you may be filled with the knowledge of His will in all spiritual wisdom and understanding" (Colossians 1:9).

True knowledge also involves developing a Christ-centered worldview. Our worldview is the lens through which we see and interpret life through the influence of family, culture, and experience. It develops so subtly that we assume what we see is all there is. Gaining true knowledge resembles going to the doctor for an eye exam and discovering myopia or astigmatism. Just as the eye doctor applies corrective lenses to clear our physical vision, so the Spirit of God applies the truth of Scripture as spiritual lenses to correct our spiritual vision.

With the lens of true knowledge, things we didn't see or were fuzzy become clear. Life changes from black and white to color; from two dimensions to three. We begin to see life from God's perspective resulting in insight and wisdom.

This week begin to memorize Colossians 1:9 as you ask God to increase our true knowledge.

Colossians 1:4-12

RECORD

REFLECT

RESPOND

1 John 4:1-8

READ

RECORD

REFLECT

RESPOND

READ

RECORD

REFLECT

RESPOND

Write it out *(Copy it from your Bible)*

_____
_____
_____
_____
_____
_____
_____

Define key words *(Use a dictionary. Page 33)*

_____
_____
_____
_____
_____
_____
_____
_____
_____
_____
_____
_____
_____
_____

Say it again *(Put it in your own words. Page 34)*

_____
_____
_____
_____
_____
_____
_____
_____
_____
_____
_____

_____
_____
_____
_____
_____
_____
_____
_____
_____
_____
_____
_____
_____
_____
_____
_____
_____
_____
_____
_____
_____

LIFE APPLICATION _____
_____
_____
_____
_____
_____

Is there a.....

S in to avoid?

P romise to claim?

E xample to follow?

C ommand to obey?

K nowledge to believe

CONNECTION

"Because we care, what do we need to know?"

EXPLORATION

"Because God's Word is true, what are you discovering?"

APPLICATION

"Because God's Word is relevant, what is He telling you to do?"

INTERCESSION

"Because God cares, how can we support you in prayer?"

65

True knowledge is similar to wisdom. Wisdom can be described as a sound course of action based on knowledge. True knowledge, like wisdom, is more than knowing facts. It involves the relationship of facts, understanding, insight, and application developed in the context of our relationship with Christ. Playing baseball is far different than memorizing facts about baseball.

"Blessed is the man who finds wisdom, the man who gains understanding, for she is more profitable than silver and yields better returns than gold. She is more precious than rubies; nothing you desire can compare with her. Long life is in her right hand; in her left hand are riches and honor. Her ways are pleasant ways, and all her paths are peace" (Proverbs 3:13-17).

Wisdom and true knowledge are available but not automatic with age or experience. Wisdom must be valued, pursued, held onto, and treasured. A child starts with foolishness, and that foolishness remains in him as a man if not replaced. Wisdom marks maturity.

True knowledge also takes humility, surrender, and steps of faith. It takes the admission that our ways are not God's ways and our thoughts are not his thoughts. It requires submitting our mind and will to the final authority of Scripture. "It seems to me" is replaced by "what does the Scripture say?" True knowledge cannot exist in a biblical vacuum.

Don't make the mistake of equating professional success with true knowledge. You may be a respected leader in your professional field but an infant in spiritual understanding. A respected church leader may have served faithfully for years with a drawer full of perfect attendance badges and plaques of recognition. However, because he never really pursued an authentic, deepening relationship with Christ, he remains shallow in spiritual understanding.

Don't be satisfied with experience if it doesn't include spiritual understanding. Make every effort to add spiritual understanding to your faith with humility and intentionality.

READ

RECORD

REFLECT

RESPOND

Ephesians 1:15-23

READ

RECORD

REFLECT

RESPOND

RECORD

REFLECT

RESPOND

Write it out *(Copy it from your Bible)*

_____
_____
_____
_____
_____
_____
_____

Break it down *(See, Search & So What? Page 34)*

_____
_____
_____
_____
_____
_____
_____
_____
_____
_____
_____
_____
_____
_____
_____

Find the bottom line *(The main principle. Page 35)*

_____
_____
_____
_____
_____
_____
_____
_____
_____
_____
_____

SUMMARIZE KEY IDEAS

_____
_____
_____
_____
_____
_____
_____
_____
_____
_____
_____
_____
_____
_____
_____
_____
_____
_____
_____

LIFE APPLICATION _____
_____
_____
_____
_____

Is there a.....
  S in to avoid?
  P romise to claim?
  E xample to follow?
  C ommand to obey?
  K nowledge to believe

"Because we care, what do we need to know?"

EXPLORATION

"Because God's Word is true, what are you discovering?"

APPLICATION

"Because God's Word is relevant, what is He telling you to do?"

INTERCESSION

"Because God cares, how can we support you in prayer?"

The third trait we are to add to our faith is translated "self control, temperance, self discipline or self mastery." The term self control implies self government. A person is self controlled when he chooses to do what he *should do* rather than what is *easy to do*. Self control implies opposing forces demanding a response. A man with self control demonstrates the ability to follow through with the right decision.

Self control provides a critical form of personal defense. "Like a city whose walls are broken down, is a man who lacks self control" (Proverbs 25:28).

Self control is like the protective walls of an ancient city. Walls kept out invaders and gave security to its citizens. Without them, the people were vulnerable, exposed, and defenseless, as we are without self control. It provides the safety net and support system for a life of virtue.

Self control is most evident when our response is contrary to what would be expected or natural. When Jesus was unjustly accused and beaten, he did not defend himself or strike back (as he could have). His response was not caused by passivity or fear but self control. He had the power to defend himself, but he chose to submit. Self control requires making the right decision and the self government to carry it out.

Each of us desires greater self control. We struggle with the "over" issues: over-eating, over-spending, over-reacting, etc. We console ourselves with victim excuses that blame our past ancestry, circumstances, or even our genes. We do everything except take personal responsibility for our decisions.

Our key verse for self control is 2 Timothy 1:7, "For God did not give us a spirit of timidity, but a spirit of power, of love and of self-discipline." Paul destroys our excuses by reminding us of the resources we have in Christ. We are no longer limited by our personality, background, or circumstances because we are recipients of God's own Spirit. He lives in us to empower us to live a life of self control. No more excuses. The real issue is not "can I?" but "will I?"

READ

RECORD

REFLECT

RESPOND

2 Timothy 1:1-11

Day 1

RECORD

REFLECT

RESPOND

READ

RECORD

REFLECT

RESPOND

READ

RECORD

REFLECT

RESPOND

Write it out *(Copy it from your Bible)*

_____
_____
_____
_____
_____
_____
_____

Define key words *(Use a dictionary. Page 33)*

_____
_____
_____
_____
_____
_____
_____
_____
_____
_____
_____
_____
_____
_____
_____
_____

Say it again *(Put it in your own words. Page 34)*

_____
_____
_____
_____
_____
_____
_____
_____
_____
_____
_____
_____

SUMMARIZE KEY IDEAS

LIFE APPLICATION _____

Is there a.....
  S in to avoid?
  P romise to claim?
  E xample to follow?
  C ommand to obey?
  K nowledge to believe

"Because we care, what do we need to know?"

EXPLORATION

"Because God's Word is true, what are you discovering?"

APPLICATION

"Because God's Word is relevant, what is He telling you to do?"

INTERCESSION

"Because God cares, how can we support you in prayer?"

Self control implies training and discipline. Serious athletes know the value of discipline. For example, to succeed a runner knows he must exercise discipline over his mind and body. To achieve his goal he must discipline his diet, schedule, and priorities.

Paul applied the same principle to his life of faith. His goal was to complete his spiritual race. He knew that many begin well but finish poorly; many are disqualified for disregarding God's rules. You may know some. Somewhere along the race they drifted or stepped out of bounds. They didn't intend to. They didn't start out the day planning to fail, but they did. Paul, knowing this danger, said, "But I discipline my body and make it my slave, lest possibly, after I have preached to others, I myself should be disqualified" (I Corinthians 9:27).

Self control doesn't mean becoming robotic but it does mean mastery over self. Out of all God's creation, man is uniquely given the ability to choose the proper response at the proper time. We are not limited by instinct, we can make choices. Self control is choosing what is right, appropriate, or valuable at the proper time.

Self control also means developing new habits or patterns of action. A surgeon trains his hands to handle the various instruments of his profession so that during an actual operation, he can focus on what he is doing rather than how he is doing it. In our journey of faith self control works the same way. It turns spiritual practices (prayer, AWG, Scripture memory) into habits of the heart which set us free to focus on the journey. These habits are not the goal but the means to the goal of a deepening relationship with Christ and a daily walk that honors him.

As you reflect on the trait of self control, do some personal assessment. Are there areas where your wall of self control is broken down? Are you vulnerable? If so, don't excuse yourself as a victim. Ask God to unleash his power for self control and repair your wall.

RECORD

REFLECT

RESPOND

RECORD

REFLECT

RESPOND

RECORD

REFLECT

RESPOND

READ

RECORD

REFLECT

RESPOND

PLANNED MEDITATION

Write it out (Copy it from your Bible)

Break it down (See, Search & So What? Page 34)

Find the bottom line (The main principle. Page 35)

SUMMARIZE KEY IDEAS

LIFE APPLICATION

Is there a.....

S in to avoid?

P romise to claim?

E xample to follow?

C ommand to obey?

K nowledge to believe

CONNECTION

"Because we care, what do we need to know?"

EXPLORATION

"Because God's Word is true, what are you discovering?"

APPLICATION

"Because God's Word is relevant, what is He telling you to do?"

INTERCESSION

"Because God cares, how can we support you in prayer?"

The root word for perseverance means "to abide or continue in" (John 15:5). But the word Peter uses to describe our next trait is a stronger form and means to continue joyfully and hopefully under adversity or pressure. Perseverance is an active, involved, and determined response to adversity. Patience and endurance are synonyms but are more passive. Perseverance actively holds onto something. It has an anchor point and a level of expectancy.

However, perseverance is not just "bull dog" tenacity. The Christ-like trait of perseverance comes from the humble willingness to endure opposition by exercising our faith in the sovereignty of God and in his promises. It involves a commitment to his plan and purpose, regardless of how uncomfortable or inconvenient that may be.

Paul encourages believers in the early churches to persevere in Kingdom work by putting their hope in God. "Therefore, my beloved brethren, be steadfast, immovable, always abounding in the work of the Lord, knowing that your toil is not in vain in the Lord" (1 Corinthians 15:58).

They, like us, must have wondered if their Kingdom work was significant. Was it making a difference? Maybe the opposition appeared to be winning. Maybe they were tired. Paul's challenge to them (and us) is to take hold of the promises of God and persevere.

Scripture also links perseverance with the development of our faith and godliness. "And not only this, but we also exult in our tribulations, knowing that tribulation brings about perseverance; and perseverance, proven character; and proven character, hope" (Romans 5:3-4).

In a culture where most things are marketed as "easy, quick, and instant", perseverance is strangely out of place. When "Why wait?" is our mantra, we undervalue or ignore those things that take time. We landscape our lawns with bushes rather than oak trees. We settle for information rather than character. We spend rather than save. We want a feel good spirituality rather than the godliness that comes through perseverance.

READ

RECORD

REFLECT

RESPOND

RECORD

REFLECT

RESPOND

James 1:1-8

Day 3

93

Romans 5:1-5

RECORD

REFLECT

RESPOND

Write it out (Copy it from your Bible)

_____
_____
_____
_____
_____
_____

Define key words (Use a dictionary. Page 33)

_____
_____
_____
_____
_____
_____
_____
_____
_____
_____
_____
_____
_____
_____

Say it again (Put it in your own words. Page 34)

_____
_____
_____
_____
_____
_____
_____
_____
_____
_____
_____
_____

SUMMARIZE KEY IDEAS

_____
_____
_____
_____
_____
_____
_____
_____
_____
_____
_____
_____
_____
_____
_____
_____
_____
_____
_____
_____

LIFE APPLICATION _____
_____
_____
_____
_____

Is there a.....
  S in to avoid?   _____
  P romise to claim? _____
  E xample to follow? _____
  C ommand to obey?   _____
  K nowledge to believe _____

CONNECTION

"Because we care, what do we need to know?"

EXPLORATION

"Because God's Word is true, what are you discovering?"

APPLICATION

"Because God's Word is relevant, what is He telling you to do?"

INTERCESSION

"Because God cares, how can we support you in prayer?"

97

Christ-like perseverance is not reluctant but willing. It endures out of a growing love for God and others. Paul describes his tests of perseverance as afflictions, hardships, and distresses (2 Corinthians 6). He refers to them without a sense of bitterness, anger or remorse because he was simply following the model of Jesus. Paul saw perseverance in the life of Christ and expected it as a normal part of the life of faith.

"Now may the God who gives perseverance and encouragement grant you to be of the same mind with one another according to Christ Jesus" (Romans 15:5).

Serving others in the cause of Christ requires hopeful perseverance. Luke 15 contains three parables about seeking something lost: lost sheep, lost coin, and a lost son. Each story demonstrates the perseverance of the seeker: the shepherd, the woman, and the father. We are often ineffective seekers of lost people because we lack perseverance. Jesus said that the shepherd looked for his lost sheep "until he found it." The woman sought her lost coin "carefully until she found it." Seeking lost people today takes more than having the right answers; it takes persistent love.

Godly persistence requires anchoring our hope in God's promises for the future. It does not expect to always receive the fulfillment now or even in this life-time. The faith heroes of Hebrews 11 are men and women who persisted through difficulty because of their hope for the future. "All these people were still living by faith when they died. They did not receive the things promised; they only saw them and welcomed them from a distance. And they admitted that they were aliens and strangers on earth" (Hebrews 11:13).

The life of faith requires hopeful perseverance to the end. All past and future heroes of faith share the common trait of hopeful perseverance. Those who end their lives well will be those who know what it means to add to their faith "hopeful persistence."

1 Peter 2:18-25

RECORD

REFLECT

RESPOND

RECORD

REFLECT

RESPOND

Revelation 2:1-7

1 Thessalonians 1:1-10

Write it out *(Copy it from your Bible)*

Break it down *(See, Search & So What? Page 34)*

Find the bottom line *(The main principle. Page 35)*

SUMMARIZE KEY IDEAS

LIFE APPLICATION _____

Is there a.....
   S in to avoid?
   P romise to claim?
   E xample to follow?
   C ommand to obey?
   K nowledge to believe

"Because we care, what do we need to know?"

EXPLORATION

"Because God's Word is true, what are you discovering?"

APPLICATION

"Because God's Word is relevant, what is He telling you to do?"

INTERCESSION

"Because God cares, how can we support you in prayer?"

The next quality Peter tells us to add to our faith is translated "godliness, reverence, respect, awe, or reverent wonder." Reverent wonder is described as "character and conduct determined by the principle of love and fear of God." In earlier history it was called piety. This trait combines reverence and holy living or reverence with affection and devotion. It is the response of the soul to the majesty and glory of God that says, "Wow!"

Reverent wonder seeks to know God as he is; not like we want him to be. We too often want God to fit into our mental box so we can manipulate him for our advantage. We want a God we can control or at least One who is comfortable. We tend to see God as like us only better. Remember, we are made in God's image; not he in ours.

There is a scene in CS Lewis's story "The Lion, the Witch and the Wardrobe" in which the children are trying to understand the nature of Aslan, the great lion of Narnia. Peter cautiously asks Mr. Beaver, "But is he safe?" "Safe?" replies Mr. Beaver, "Who said anything about safe? Of course he isn't safe. But he is good."

During the 1980s, Oldsmobile tried to recapture its declining share of the automobile market by reinventing itself. In 1988 it came out with the slogan, "It's not your father's Oldsmobile." They tried to reposition the elegant Olds as something different than what it was. It was the beginning of the end. After a 100 year history, the Oldsmobile was phased out in 2004. In our attempt to reinvent or remarket God to a declining audience, are we in danger of reinventing God to fit our culture? Are we in danger of domesticating the Lion of Judah and emasculating the King of Kings?

Stop and look; wonder and gaze at the God of glory. Reverent wonder (godliness) is more than knowing about God; it is the experience of God. Let what you see express itself in how you live and relate to your ordinary, go-to-work world this week.

1 Timothy 4:6-10

RECORD

REFLECT

RESPOND

READ

RECORD

REFLECT

RESPOND

RECORD

REFLECT

RESPOND

READ

RECORD

REFLECT

RESPOND

Write it out (Copy it from your Bible)

Define key words (Use a dictionary. Page 33)

Say it again (Put it in your own words. Page 34)

CHECK THE MAP

_____
_____
_____
_____
_____
_____
_____
_____
_____
_____
_____
_____
_____
_____
_____
_____
_____
_____
_____

LIFE APPLICATION _____
_____
_____
_____
_____

Is there a.....
  S in to avoid?
  P romise to claim?
  E xample to follow?
  C ommand to obey?
  K nowledge to believe

CONNECTION

"Because we care, what do we need to know?"

EXPLORATION

"Because God's Word is true, what are you discovering?"

APPLICATION

"Because God's Word is relevant, what is He telling you to do?"

INTERCESSION

"Because God cares, how can we support you in prayer?"

Reverent wonder or godliness is also expressed by the phrase "The fear of the Lord." This concept is found through-out the entire Bible from Genesis to Revelation. The fear of God does not mean that we experience terror, that we shrink back at his presence, or that we are afraid of his wrath. Instead the fear of God is a reverence or veneration for our loving Father and Creator. It is the awesome respect that allows us to come into his presence boldly (Heb 4:16) but never casually.

When we are controlled by the fear of the Lord rather than circumstances or other people, we find it protects us from redefining God's nature and distorting his love. It prevents us from treating God casually or living life carelessly.

The godliness or reverent wonder that Peter refers to, seeks not only to know him but to please him. It is an attitude of grateful love and constant devotion. It is a response that honors, respects, and responds to the will of God. There is no godliness without responsiveness. Jesus demonstrated his godliness by his submission to the will of his Father. "I have glorified you on earth having accomplished the work you have given me to do" (John 17:4 NASB).

When we are gripped by reverent wonder, we will find our-selves speechless; unable to defend our sinfulness or to justify our self centeredness. When the eyes of our soul see God re-vealed in his power, greatness, love, compassion, and creative genius, we can only stand in awe and humbly ask, "Lord, what do you want from me?"

If we want to gaze in reverent wonder at the nature of God, we have only to look at Jesus. "In the past God spoke to our forefathers through the prophets at many times and in various ways, but in these last days he has spoken to us by his Son, whom he appointed heir of all things, and through whom he made the universe. The Son is the radiance of God's glory and the exact representation of his being, sustaining all things by his powerful word" (Hebrews 1:1-3).

READ

RECORD

REFLECT

RESPOND

RECORD

REFLECT

RESPOND

READ

RECORD

Proverbs 1:7; 3:7; 8:13; 14:26-27; 16:6;
19:23; 22:4; 23:17

Day 3

REFLECT

RESPOND

RECORD

REFLECT

RESPOND

Write it out (Copy it from your Bible)

Break it down (See, Search & So What? Page 34)

Find the bottom line (The main principle. Page 35)

CHECK THE MAP

LIFE APPLICATION _____

Is there a.....
S in to avoid?
P romise to claim?
E xample to follow?
C ommand to obey?
K nowledge to believe

"Because we care, what do we need to know?"

EXPLORATION

"Because God's Word is true, what are you discovering?"

APPLICATION

"Because God's Word is relevant, what is He telling you to do?"

INTERCESSION

"Because God cares, how can we support you in prayer?"

The final trait that Peter tells us to add to our faith is love. The New Testament expresses love with two different Greek words: phileo and agape. The former is a brotherly, family love and the latter, a spiritual, unmerited love. Peter refers to them as "brotherly love" and "love." Both kinds of love are translated into our English Bibles as simply "love."

Phileo (brotherly) love is the positive response to qualities of kindness, goodwill, and benevolence that makes a relationship mutually attractive. It is a strong friendship love that is found in companions who find pleasure in each other's company. Brotherly love is most often used to describe how we are to respond to those in the family of faith. It is in that sense a family love.

In the New Testament, agape love refers to the constant and undeserving love of God expressed towards man. This is a love of grace as opposed to merit. God chose to love (agape) us. And the amazing, humbling truth is that God loves us without any merit on our part (Romans 5:8).

This week each AWG passage uses both terms for love: phileo and agape. In the memory verse for the week, Peter tells the early believers that they did well in choosing to love (phileo) the family of faith, but he says, don't stop there. Now take love to a higher plane and fervently love (agape) each other from the heart. In the next two sessions of *His Nature*, we will refer to both kinds of love under the heading "Genuine Love."

"Now that you have purified yourselves by obeying the truth so that you have sincere love for your brothers, love one another deeply, from the heart" (1 Peter 1:22).

The act of adding genuine love to our faith is not born out of emotion, but it is a choice that requires action. As you consider the people in your natural, life networks, is God pointing out someone who needs your love in action this week?

1 Peter 1:17-25

RECORD

REFLECT

RESPOND

Romans 12:9-21

RECORD

REFLECT

RESPOND

RECORD

REFLECT

RESPOND

Write it out *(Copy it from your Bible)*

Define key words *(Use a dictionary. Page 33)*

Say it again *(Put it in your own words. Page 34)*

CHECK THE MAP

_____
_____
_____
_____
_____
_____
_____
_____
_____
_____
_____
_____
_____
_____
_____
_____
_____
_____
_____
_____
_____

LIFE APPLICATION _____
_____
_____
_____
_____

Is there a.....
  S in to avoid?
  P romise to claim?
  E xample to follow?
  C ommand to obey?
  K nowledge to believe

FORUM DISCUSSION

CONNECTION

"Because we care, what do we need to know?"

EXPLORATION

"Because God's Word is true, what are you discovering?"

APPLICATION

"Because God's Word is relevant, what is He telling you to do?"

INTERCESSION

"Because God cares, how can we support you in prayer?"

Love, to be genuine, must reveal itself in action. Genuine love for God expresses itself in obedience.   Real love is not simply a belief but a response. Jesus said to his disciples, "Whoever has my commands and obeys them, he is the one who loves me" (John 14:21). Genuine love for God responds by knowing and doing his will; not reluctantly but eagerly.

Jesus said the greatest commandment in the Jewish Scripture was to love God with everything you have and the second was to love others as yourself. The Old Testament standard for loving others was self love. In the New Testament, Christ raised the bar. "A new command I give you: love one another. As I have loved you, so you must love one another" (John 13:34).

Loving others was not a new command. But loving others in the same way Christ loved them, was new. Down through history, the hallmark trait of men of faith has been their sacrificial and constant love for others. Genuine love doesn't wither in the heat of opposition or ingratitude. It first responds to God; then to the family of faith; and ultimately to the world.

Bernard of Clarevoix, a medieval French monk, wrote that mature love develops through three stages:
1. Loving God for my sake
2. Loving God for his sake
3. Loving others for God's sake

Too often we stop at #1 ("benefits" level). We love God as long as he blesses our lives, expands our careers, and makes us happy. But Christ is not satisfied with his disciples remaining childish in their love. He desires their love to be mature; to go beyond the narrow confines of self absorbed interest and to embrace his heart.

Adding genuine love to our faith is a journey from focusing on self to focusing on others. One of the greatest blocks to our spiritual maturity, is our unwillingness to give our lives away for the sake of others.

"By this all men will know that you are my disciples, if you love one another" (John 13:35).

READ

RECORD

REFLECT

RESPOND

RECORD

REFLECT

RESPOND

READ

RECORD

REFLECT

RESPOND

1 John 2:1-11

Write it out *(Copy it from your Bible)*

_____
_____
_____
_____
_____
_____

Break it down *(See, Search & So What? Page 34)*

_____
_____
_____
_____
_____
_____
_____
_____
_____
_____
_____
_____
_____
_____
_____
_____

Find the bottom line *(The main principle. Page 35)*

_____
_____
_____
_____
_____
_____
_____
_____
_____
_____
_____

SUMMARIZE KEY IDEAS

_____
_____
_____
_____
_____
_____
_____
_____
_____
_____
_____
_____
_____
_____
_____
_____
_____
_____
_____
_____

LIFE APPLICATION _____
_____
_____
_____
_____

Is there a.....
   S in to avoid?
   P romise to claim?
   E xample to follow?
   C ommand to obey?
   K nowledge to believe

CONNECTION

"Because we care, what do we need to know?"

EXPLORATION

"Because God's Word is true, what are you discovering?"

APPLICATION

"Because God's Word is relevant, what is He telling you to do?"

INTERCESSION

"Because God cares, how can we support you in prayer?"

HIGHQUEST

His Nature

APPENDIX

As you begin HighQuest II, it will be beneficial to Ipractice together this new life skill of Planned Meditation (PM). To do this, follow the practice plan below and fill out the Planned Meditation forms on pages 142 and 143. The verse you will use is 2 Peter 1:4. This verse is from one of the passages you will look at in your AWG this week.

One of the study skills you will use is defining key words in the verse. Because you probably do not have a dictionary with you, the definitions for key words in 2 Peter 1:4 are listed on the next page. Normally a good English dictionary will be adequate for gaining insight into key words. You may also like to use a Bible dictionary like *Vines Complete Expository Dictionary of New Testament Words* or *Vincent Word Studies*. In *His Nature* there are two parts to the planned meditation. You will do one part each week. In this practice exercise, you will do both at once.

Planned Meditation Practice (page 142-143)

1. **"Write it out."** Copy 2 Peter 1:4 from your Bible.

2. **"Define key words."** Identify the key words in the verse and write down (highlight in this exercise) definitions. Refer to the definitions listed for you on the next page. Share your insights with the group.

3. **"Say it again."** Write out 2 Peter 1:4 in your own words using insights from your definition of key words. This becomes your "paraphrase" of the verse. Share your paraphrase with your group.

4. **"Break it down."** Review the explanation of how to break it down on page 34. Write down a few of your observations. As a group, share insights and observations from the verse.

5. **"Find the bottom line."** Write down a summary of what this verse means to you. Have a few men in the group share their summary with the others.

Precious
1. Of high cost or worth; valuable 2. Highly esteemed; cherished 3. Dear; beloved

Promise
1. A declaration assuring that one will or will not do something; a vow 2. Something promised

Participate
1. To take part in something 2. To share in something

Divine
1. Having the nature of or being a deity 2. Heavenly; perfect

Nature
1. The essential characteristics and qualities of a person or thing 2. The fundamental character of a person

Escape
1. To break loose from confinement; get free; escape from jail
2. To avoid a serious or unwanted outcome

Corruption
1. Lack of integrity or honesty use of a position of trust for dishonest gain 2. In a state of progressive putrefaction
3. Moral perversion; impairment of virtue and moral principles; moral degeneracy

World
1. The system of life (beliefs, values, ethics and practices) marked by self-reliance and independence from God

Part A: 2 Peter 1:4

Write it out *(Copy it from your Bible)*

_____
_____
_____
_____
_____
_____
_____
_____

Define key words *(Use a dictionary. Page 33)*

_____
_____
_____
_____
_____
_____
_____
_____
_____
_____
_____
_____
_____
_____
_____
_____
_____

Say it again *(Put it in your own words. Page 34)*

_____
_____
_____
_____
_____
_____
_____
_____
_____
_____
_____
_____
_____

Part B: 2 Peter 1:4

Write it out *(Copy it from your Bible)*

_____
_____
_____
_____
_____
_____

Break it down *(See, Search & So What? Page 34)*

_____
_____
_____
_____
_____
_____
_____
_____
_____
_____
_____
_____
_____
_____

Find the bottom line *(The main principle. Page 35)*

_____
_____
_____
_____
_____
_____
_____
_____
_____

PLANNED MEDITATION

The Appointment With God life skill is a spiritual habit or discipline that will equip you for a lifetime of walking with Christ. Once you learn how to use it, you can adapt it to fit your quest for knowing Christ no matter where you are along your spiritual journey.

Meeting regularly with Christ is like using a compass. A compass has been standard equipment for travelers for centuries. A compass is especially critical for anyone climbing in the mountains because it gives a reliable point of reference. It allows a climber to keep on track no matter what the conditions are around him. Likewise, your AWG will allow you to check your spiritual position, get your bearings and chart your course as you keep your eyes and heart on Christ.

An AWG is a regular, daily time when you relate with Christ through his Word and prayer. This spiritual discipline has been called by many names, but it has consistently proven essential throughout Christian history in every age and culture.

We are accustomed to making appointments for just about everything. Appointments insure that intentions get carried out. Making an appointment helps us commit to a particular course of action. We often intend to get time alone with God but fail to pull it off. We think it's a good idea and even have it on our "do list". But until we get it on our appointment calendar, it remains just a good intention.

Establishing the habit of meeting with God on a regular basis is foundational to developing a deeper relationship with Christ. Friendships develop with dialogue and shared experiences over time. Meeting in corporate worship is no substitute for individual interaction with God. Periodic time with God is not as effective as consistent time with him.

Imagine your frustration if a friend says he wants to meet with you but never shows up. The Bible presents God as intensely eager to meet with us. He waits, hopes, even calls to see if we are coming. It's time we kept the appointment. The prophet Isaiah said, "Seek the Lord while you can find him. Call on him now while he is near."

HighQuest I will teach you the basic elements of this important life skill. But it will take practice, discipline, and perseverance to make it a habit in your life.

Learning a new skill or habit is awkward initially. It usually takes a number of tries and a few falls to learn to ride a bike. At first we don't even care where we are going. Our goal is to stay vertical! But once we master the skill, we no longer think about balance or steering. We are free to keep our heads up, experience what's around us, and enjoy the journey. In the same way, mastering new spiritual skills gives us greater freedom and joy as we develop our relationship with God.

Initially you may find that 10 to 15 minutes a day is adequate for your AWG. But as you develop your relationship with Christ, your desire to spend time in his presence will increase. On the other hand, some days you will find it tough to get even 10 to 15 minutes. Don't make the mistake of measuring your relationship with Christ based on the performance of the discipline. Disciplines are necessary, but they are not a merit system with God.

Keep your eyes and heart on Christ and let the disciplines and skills become like the sails on a ship. In the same way the sails catch the wind and power the ship, so also the spiritual disciplines catch the wind of the Spirit of God. He is the power behind our quest to follow Christ.

Strategy

In order to establish a consistent AWG, you need to establish a realistic time, place and plan.

• Time

Identify a consistent time during the day when you can get alone with God. It is best to build the AWG habit

AWG EXPLANATION

around the same time each day. There is no time that is right or wrong but there is a time that will work best for you. It needs to be a time when you are alert, which may be the first thing in the day for some or at the end of the day for others. The best time for you may be over lunch or before work. Discover what works best for you and stick with it.

The length of time spent each day in an AWG is not as critical as the habit of doing it consistently. Begin with 15 minutes until it becomes a habit. Once you have developed the habit, it is easy to expand it as needed.

• Place

You need to identify a place where you can meet with God privately, regularly and free from distractions. It may be a special room or a favorite chair in your home or office. You will need to be flexible because the best place will often change as circumstances change.

• Plan

It is important to develop a simple plan that will allow an effective dialogue with Christ and promote consistency. You can enhance and modify your plan as you gain confidence. HighQuest I introduces you to a plan that has been used throughout Christian history by men and women of all ages and every culture. It is simple and can be easily adapted to changing lifestyles.

Step 1: Read

Begin your AWG by reading a passage of Scripture. It can be a few verses or a whole chapter. Usually it is best to limit the reading to a few verses in order to have time to reflect over them. The purpose of an AWG is to meet with God not to gain a lot of information. We suggest using an inexpensive Bible for your AWG. As you read over the passage several times, mark words and ideas that stand out to you.

Each week in HighQuest I, you will read five passages with a common theme. The goal is to be consistent in your AWG for at least 5 out of 7 days. Once you finish HighQuest, you can continue with your AWG using your own reading selections.

Remember the passages given are not to limit you but to start you. You may read more than suggested or not as much. The AWG is designed for you to stop and dialogue with God as he speaks through his Word. It is not designed to be a comprehensive Bible study. Rather it is designed to help you connect with Christ on a regular and personal basis – to sit as his feet and listen to his words.

Step 2: Record

Once you have read the passage over a few times, note the verse or phrase that God seems to emphasize. It may be a complete verse, a statement or a phrase. Write this out, word for word, in your AWG journal page. Recording this Biblical statement will help you focus your thoughts and listen to God. Selecting one verse or phrase helps to corral a wandering mind and sharpen your focus.

Step 3: Reflect

Stop and think about what God is saying to you from what you have recorded. Ask questions to gain insight and understanding into God's truth. For example ask "what, why, how or when" type questions. You are looking not only for what the passage says but what it means. You first record the facts (what does it say?) and then reflect to understand the implications (what does it say to me?). Remember you are putting your heart in a position to listen to God. Don't be afraid to be silent and tune in to the quiet voice of the Holy Spirit.

As you reflect, write down your ideas and thoughts on the

journal page. Often God will give you something specific that you need to apply to your life. When He does, write it down as well.

Journaling has many advantages. It helps you clarify and formulate concisely what you are hearing from God in Scripture. Thoughts take on shape and stick in your mind as you write them down. Keeping this kind of a journal becomes a way to log your journey with God. Journaling allows you to remember patterns and major lessons God is working out in your life.

Step 4: Respond
Once you have reflected on God's Word, it is important to pray over what you have just read and thought about. Write out a short 1-2 sentence prayer that expresses back to God what you have heard him say. Allow what you've read to guide your prayer time. You will also want to pray over issues and people who will be part of your day's agenda.

What People are Saying About HighQuest

Businessmen

I am living a more authentic Christian life in my home and in my business because of the effect of the HighQuest series.

Chris Miller, President LANIT Consulting, Inc., Oregon

"HighQuest" has been a blessing to our men's ministry. It has just the right balance for digging into the Scripture with a format to build strong godly relationships. The result has been a deeper relationship with God and with each other.

Bryan Gilbert, President, Alpha-Omega Industries, Missouri

Pastors

For years I struggled to get my church board members to develop a consistent devotional life with little success. The "HighQuest" materials were the first tools that brought all the elements together that helped them to develop a consistent and deeper walk with Christ. The easy to follow format, the accountability meetings, and the heart and skill development helped to connect us not only to God but to each other. We now look forward to meeting with each other to share what God is teaching us. I recommend this tool to anyone who wants a simple but powerful tool for equipping people to connect with God and each other.

John Grussi, Pastor Peninsula Christian Fellowship, California

"HighQuest" has brought simple spiritual disciplines into the hands of our men in practical ways. I see men wrestling with God, their world, and themselves in life changing ways. God is more real and closer than they had ever thought...and the Scriptures are coming alive to them in fresh ways. As a pastor I love seeing God's people grow spiritually. I am convinced that if men can grow and mature spiritually it will have a Christ-honoring impact in the home, the neighborhoods at church, and around the world.

Matt Uldrich , Director of Men's Ministry, Catalina Foothills Church, Arizona

Navigator Staff

I had been searching for an effective tool to help men develop a consistent appointment with God when I came across the "HighQuest" series. There are lots of activities for men that are all very helpful but generally, do not get men into the Word on a daily, consistent and personal basis. Using "HighQuest", I am now watching men's lives being transformed week by week as we share together what God has spoken to us about during the week.

Roger Fleming, Navigator Staff, Colorado

I have found that "HighQuest" covers the spiritual needs for discipleship training wherever a person may be in his journey. From those that are just coming to a relationship with Christ, to those who have reached a plateau in their growth, or for those who have a hunger to grow even deeper....no matter what the need, there seems to be a "HighQuest" book that is ideal for the situation. I have witnessed it changing other men's lives and have experienced it in my own. It seems to be the ideal tool for establishing a church discipleship training program.

Bill Penkethman, Navigator Staff, Missouri

About the Authors

HighQuest: Men on a Mission was developed by a team of Navigator staff who share a common vision for reaching and equipping men for Christ and His kingdom. Together they represent over 160 years of discipling experience.

Ron Bennett
Graduating from Iowa State University with a degree in Aerospace Engineering, Ron served as an officer in the US Army including a tour in Viet Nam. He has served as a Navigator staff in campus, military, and community ministries. Ron is the author of *Intentional Disciplemaking* (NavPress 2001). He coauthored *Opening the Door* and *The Adventure of Discipling Others* (NavPress 2003). Ron and his wife, Mary, wrote *Beginning the Walk* (NavPress 2005). Ron and Mary live in Kansas City where he serves as regional director for The Navigators Church Discipleship Ministry.

Larry Glabe
Larry graduated from Illinois State University with a degree in Secondary Education. He taught high school in Chicago before coming on staff with The Navigators. Larry served as The Navigator campus director at the University of Northern Iowa and the University of Missouri. He directed the Navigators Business and Professional Men's Ministry in central Missouri and served as chaplain for the Missouri Tigers. He coauthored *Opening the Door* (NavPress). Larry and his wife, Kathy, live in Columbia, MO where he serves as a spiritual coach to business men and directs The Navigator Church Discipleship Ministry in central Missouri.

Chuck Strittmatter
Chuck was raised in southwest Iowa. He served in the U.S. Navy before getting his BS degree at the University of Northern Iowa. He joined The Navigators staff and has served as campus director at Kansas State University, regional director in New England, country director of Australia, and field director for Iowa/Nebraska as well as coaching CoMission teams in Russia and Ukraine. God took Chuck home in November, 2009 after fighting cancer. He finished his course of faith well and is deeply missed. Chuck is survived by his wife, Nancy.

Bob Walz
Bob grew up in Nebraska and graduated from the University of Nebraska with a major in Zoology/Pre-Medicine. He served with The Navigators at Hosei University in Tokyo, Japan as well as led collegiate ministries at the University of Iowa, Kansas State University, and the University of Nebraska. He developed *The Field Survival Kit* which is a CD of materials for helping people minister to others. Distributed widely to service personnel in Iraq, many of the items are available at: www.navresources.com . Bob also coauthored a devotional for high school athletes called *Get in the Game*. Bob and his wife, Sandy, live in Lincoln, NE where he serves with The Navigators National Collegiate Ministry.

HighQuest
Discipleship Series

Men on a Mission

Know Christ Deeply	Reflect Christ Authentically	Share Christ Intentionally
His Works	**His Image**	**His Heart**
His Ways	**His Calling**	**His Commission**
His Glory	**His Nature**	**His Story**

Also available HighQuest: Women of Distinction series
www.highquest.info

Moral Excellence

[9] But you are a chosen people, a royal priesthood, a holy nation, a people belonging to God, that you may declare the praises of him who called you out of darkness into his wonderful light.

1 Peter 2:9 NIV

True Knowledge

[9] For this reason, since the day we heard about you, we have not stopped praying for you and asking God to fill you with the knowledge of his will through all spiritual wisdom and understanding.

Colossians 1:9 NIV

Self Control

[7] For God did not give us a spirit of timidity, but a spirit of power, of love and of self-discipline.

2 Timothy 1:7 NIV

Hopeful Perseverance

[1]Therefore, since we are surrounded by such a great cloud of witnesses, let us throw off everything that hinders and the sin that so easily entangles, and let us run with perseverance the race marked out for us.

Hebrews 12:1 NIV

Reverent Wonder

[7] Have nothing to do with godless myths and old wives' tales; rather, train yourself to be godly. [8] For physical training is of some value, but godliness has value for all things, holding promise for both the present life and the life to come.

1 Timothy 4:7-8 NIV

Genuine Love

[22] Now that you have purified yourselves by obeying the truth so that you have sincere love for your brothers, love one another deeply, from the heart.

1 Peter 1:22 NIV

Made in the USA
Lexington, KY
30 April 2019